SNEAKY TRICKS TO FOOL YOUR FRIENDS

by E. RICHARD CHURCHILL
drawings by JOYCE BEHR

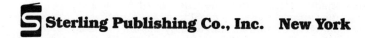

Sterling Publishing Co., Inc.   New York

This book is dedicated to
Jack and Beryl Collins,
Horley, Surrey, England,
and
Bob and Marilyn Collins,
Kings Cross, London, England,
four of the finest friends
anyone could ever have.

DIAGRAMS BY JOAN COLUMBUS

Library of Congress Cataloging-in-Publication Data

Churchill, E. Richard (Elmer Richard)
    Sneaky tricks to fool your friends.

    Includes index.
    Summary: Presents instructions with illustrations and dia-
grams, for performing a variety of tricks using math, cards, paper,
and other props.
    1. Tricks—Juvenile literature   [1. Tricks]
I. Title.
GV1548.C46   1986   792.8   86-14448
ISBN 0-8069-4806-X
ISBN 0-8069-4807-8 (lib. bdg.)

ISBN 0-8069-4808-6 (pbk.)

First Paperback Printing, 1987

Copyright © 1986 by E. Richard Churchill
Published by Sterling Publishing Co., Inc.
Two Park Avenue, New York, N.Y. 10016
Distributed in Canada by Oak Tree Press Ltd.
c/o Canadian Manda Group, P.O. Box 920, Station U
Toronto, Ontario, Canada M8Z 5P9
Distributed in the United Kingdom by Blandford Press
Link House, West Street, Poole, Dorset BH15 1LL, England
Distributed in Australia by Capricorn Ltd.
P.O. Box 665, Lane Cove, NSW 2066
Manufactured in the United States of America
All rights reserved

CONTENTS

Playing
Funny Tricks

Playing tricks on others is fun. People have been doing it for thousands of years. But it's not only fun for the trickster. The great thing is that trick victims actually enjoy being tricked. They like the surprise at the end and then they enjoy trying to figure out how the trick worked.

One of the best things about playing tricks is that one good trick usually deserves another. Very often, when you fool people with a trick, they know another trick. They show it to you and both of you have learned a new trick.

The tricks in this book are not "magic" tricks. You could use some of them in a magic act if you're into that sort of thing. But these are the tricky things people learn to do to amaze their friends. None of them will hurt the victim of the trick. Most of them are fun—or funny. Any items you need to make the trick work can usually be found around the house without any difficulty. And you won't need to practise any of these tricks more than a few times to make them work.

This is a good time for a word of advice. An old saying goes, "Don't go to the well too often."

For the trickster, the saying should be, "Don't try the same trick too many times."

Even the best card trick will eventually give itself away. Do a trick, such as "The Tattletale Chosen Card," a few times; then move on to others. Don't give people too many opportunities to figure out how your trick works—not if you want to go on being the trickiest person around, that is.

So look for this illustration as you read the book. When you see it, remember—don't repeat the trick too many times!

When you go looking for victims, always remember this: You can trick most of the people most of the time but many people can trick you much of the time. That's what it's all about!

MAKING TRICKY MOVES

Funny Money

Sooner or later all good tricksters learn something about playing tricks on others: The very simple tricks are often the most difficult for others to figure out. "Funny Money" is just this sort of trick.

All you need is a little practice and quick hands. From then on, very few people discover how it works.

Begin with a dollar bill. Hold it out in front of you with the face towards your audience. Make sure the top of the head is up.

Begin by folding the top half of the bill forward. The bill is now folded in half horizontally.

fold

Now fold it in half, bringing the end in your right hand over to the left.

Once again, fold the bill in half, bringing the end in your right hand over to the left.

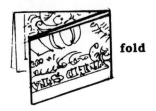

Now unfold the back half of the bill from your left hand towards your right. You are unfolding 2 layers now.

Next, unfold the front half of the bill from your right to your left. This leaves just one fold along the top.

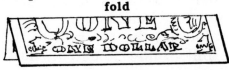

Finally, unfold the front of the bill upwards. You now have the back of the bill towards you. Your audience sees the face of the bill exactly as it was at the beginning.

Let your victims take a quick look at the face

8

on the bill. Then begin refolding the bill just as you did before. Repeat the first 4 steps: Fold the top down; fold the right side over; again fold the right side over; unfold 2 layers from left to right.

Now comes the trick. The first time you unfolded the front half of the bill from right to left. This time unfold the *back* half of the bill from right to left.

When you do the last step and unfold the bill upwards, something has happened. The face on the bill is now upside down.

Work on this alone until the 6 steps are easy for you. Practise doing the fifth step quickly and smoothly. Now you can make the head come out right side up or upside down, whichever you wish.

Since you do the folds quickly and because the change at step 5 is so difficult to spot, you can do this trick again and again without having people catch on.

As with many good tricks, this one is so simple it fools almost everyone!

The Tricky Dime

If you don't mind what others say when you trick them, try this one.

Place 2 pennies and a dime in a row, like this.

Then say: "Without touching the dime I can put it to the right of both pennies."

Just to keep your victim from really thinking about how this might be done, you can add such comments as these: "I won't hit the table. I won't tip the table. I won't push the dime with a straw or a pencil or anything like that. I won't even blow on the dime."

The trick is really sneaky. It is also so simple, you can expect cries of, "Fake! Fraud! Cheat!" If you're going to be a real trickster, however, you'll just have to get used to the fact that people are jealous of your skills.

You said you wouldn't touch the dime but would put it to the right of both pennies. Move the right-hand penny from where it is to the left of the other penny. Now look at the arrangement. The dime is to the right of both pennies.

Aren't you the tricky one!

Pretty Sneaky

The first part of this trick is just a good test of logic and planning. The second part is downright sneaky. That's what makes it such a great trick.

Arrange 5 empty glasses as shown below. (The numbers are there just to help explain how to do the trick.)

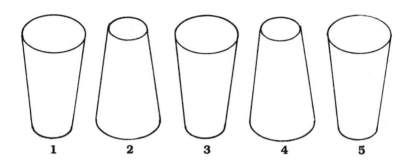

"Here's the trick," you tell your audience. "I am going to turn over 2 glasses at a time. I will do this 3 times. At the end of 3 turns, all 5 glasses will be right side up."

This doesn't sound all that difficult, so no one will act wildly impressed. Don't let this bother you. Just show everyone that you can do what you said you'd do.

Turn over glasses 1 and 4.

Turn over glasses 2 and 5.

Turn over glasses 1 and 5.

That's all there is to it. All 5 glasses are now sitting with their tops up.

You may want to say something like, "I told you I could do it."

While you're talking, begin rearranging the glasses. If anyone says something about how easy the trick was, you have a victim.

Otherwise, when the glasses are set up again, dare someone to do what you just did in 3 moves. Since it seems so easy, a victim will volunteer.

Strangely enough, *it is impossible for another person to repeat what they just saw you do.* No matter how many times people try, the trick won't work.

When you are asked for a repeat performance, you have to decide whether to risk giving away the trick or not. If you set up the glasses *after* someone has failed, the chances are good you won't get caught. This is up to you.

Here is the sneaky part of this trick. When you position the glasses for someone else, always arrange them like this.

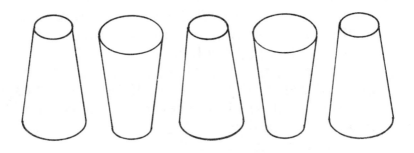

To most people, this arrangement looks exactly like the one you began with. Of course, it isn't, which is what makes the trick work.

If you decide to risk showing the solution again, keep up a steady stream of talk while you set up the glasses properly. Your talk may help to distract your audience from noticing how the glasses are arranged.

Changed—but Still the Same

Set out 5 coins in this arrangement. Or make up a new arrangement you like better.

"Here's the trick," you tell your friend and victim. "I want you to take away 2 coins from this group. Then I want you to add 3 coins so that they look just the way they do now."

"This is really tricky," you may want to add.

It does not take most people long to realize what you have asked seems impossible. Some clever person may end up putting one coin on top of another. If that happens, all you have to do is to pretend to sight along the top of the desk.

"Nope," you can say. "It doesn't look the same from here."

When you're ready to prove this trick can be done, remind your victim that you said it was really tricky.

Move any 2 coins to a new place on the table. This is the first part of the trick. Now add the 3 coins you did not move to the 2 you did move. You have completed the second part of the trick.

Don't pay any attention to those who say you tricked them. They are just jealous of your skill in tricking people!

Ready, Set, Jump

Some tricks work best on people who think they are wonderful math students. Others are designed for great athletes. This one is for the athletes.

Stand in the middle of a room and pretend to

practise jumping backwards. Don't do it very well. It won't take long for your victim to start feeling superior and show you how well he or she can jump. Or your victim may just begin to make fun of your attempts. Either way you have hooked the victim. That's what counts.

You might just want to ask your victim to show you how to jump backwards. You might want to pretend you resent being kidded about your lack of ability. Take the approach that suits you best.

For instance, you may say, "Sure. You can jump backwards when there's nothing to jump over. I'll bet if I put this book on the floor you can't jump over it backwards." Hold up a small book.

What athlete can turn down a challenge like that?

"Look," you may go on, "I don't want to make you look bad. But I know if I put this book down you can't jump over it backwards."

By now your victim is ready to jump the moon if only given the chance.

"Let's get this straight. I say I can put the book down on the floor and you can't jump over it backwards. Just one thing. After I put it on the floor, you can't move it. Not even an inch. Is it a deal?"

Of course it's a deal.

Walk to the nearest corner in the room and put the book in that corner. Make certain it touches both walls. Then step back and point to the book.

You may even wish to say something pleasant such as, "We are waiting," or "Happy landing."

Jump Across the Room

Before everyone has recovered from finding it is impossible to jump backwards over a book, pull this one on them.

"I can jump across the room." This is sure to grab their attention.

Make sure it is a fairly big room you are talking about.

Everyone knows this is another trick. After all you just set up an athlete who thought he or she could jump backwards.

Unless someone is pretty sharp you'll be able to pull this trick off just as easily as the backwards jump.

You are sure to be asked to make your move.

When you are challenged to jump across the room, just walk from one side of the room to the other. Then jump up and down a few times. You have jumped across the room just as you said you would.

You may want to say something such as, "See, it isn't all that hard. You can probably do it with a little practice."

Move
One Coin

Some of the best tricks are the most simple. When a trick looks impossible and then turns out to be quite easy, it becomes a great trick. This is just that kind of trick.

Place 4 coins on the table as shown here:

#1

#2

#3

Then say something like this: "By moving only one of these coins to a new position I can make 2 rows of 3 coins in each row."

Obviously, this seems impossible. As it is now there is one row of 3 coins and one of 2. It doesn't look as if anybody could make 2 rows of 3 coins each by moving only one coin.

Let your victim think this one over. Allow him or her to experiment by moving coins from one place to another.

When he or she is convinced there is no way in the world to do this trick you are ready to make your move.

Just pick up coin#1 and place it on top of coin

#3. Now there are 3 coins in each of the 2 rows. For variety, you may wish to put coin #2 on top of coin #3 instead. The result is the same.

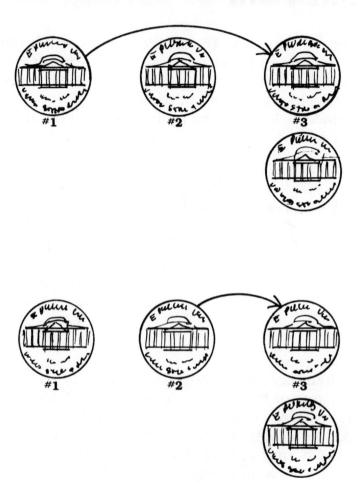

A Person Could Die of Thirst

Here's a good one to tone down hotshots who act as if they know more than anyone else.

Fill a glass partly full of water, a soft drink, or whatever. Place a saucer or salad plate on top of it. Then stand a second glass (an empty one) on the saucer. Hand this to your victim so he or she holds the bottom glass.

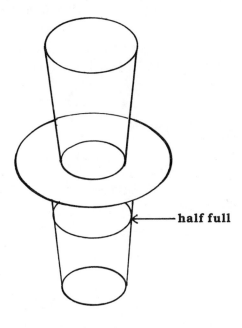

half full

You say: "Don't touch either the top glass or the saucer with your hands, lips, teeth, or any other part of your body. You may touch anything else in the room but not those 2 items. Don't ask anyone else to touch the top glass or saucer until you're willing to admit you can't do this trick."

What you have to do is take a drink out of the bottom glass. But you must not let go of that bottom glass until you figure out how to take a drink from it."

Now you can give your victim a sly smile. "Of course, if you can't figure out how to do it, I'll be happy to show you."

As is the case with most tricks, the solution is so easy and so obvious everyone wonders why they didn't see it first.

Place 2 boxes or 2 stacks of books or any other objects side by side. Leave just enough room so you can lower the bottom glass between them. Make certain the edges of the saucer or salad plate touch each stack firmly. Also, be sure the boxes or books are the same height.

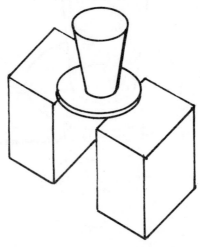

Once you have the saucer firmly set on top of the boxes, remove the bottom glass and take a drink.

When someone says, "That's simple" or "That's easy," don't get upset. Just smile. After all, if the answer was so simple, why didn't they think of it?

Coins
on the Rim

Balance 2 coins on the rim of a glass as shown here.

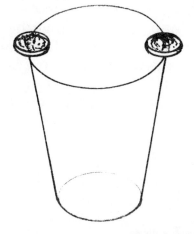

Set your victim up by saying, "I can take both those coins from the rim of the glass at the same time. I will touch the coins with only one finger and my thumb. I won't tip the glass. I won't drop the coins. I will finish this trick holding the two coins between my thumb and finger."

Most people have to try this trick first. Let any and all give it a try. The chances are no one will be able to see how you are going to do what you say.

Don't allow the glass to be moved. Make sure everyone understands the 2 coins must be removed from the rim at the same time.

When your victims admit this seems impossible, the spotlight is on you.

Hold the glass firmly with one hand. (This is done so that it doesn't go scooting across the table while everyone has a good laugh at your expense.)

Place the thumb of your other hand on one coin. Put a finger on the second coin. Snap both coins down onto the outside edge of the glass. Hold them firmly so that they don't slip away.

Pull your thumb and finger towards the front of the glass. Snap the coins together and take them away from the glass. Then accept any congratulations your victims may offer.

Practise this tricky trick before trying it in public. It's not hard to do, but you have to do it correctly.

The Dollar Is Still Strong

A favorite way for many pranksters to introduce a trick is to pretend they don't know what they're talking about. That may be just the way to get this puzzling trick started. You'll need more than one person in the group.

Hold up a dollar bill and pretend to study it carefully. You may even give it a few tugs as though you're trying to see how strong the paper is.

"I read that the dollar is weaker than it used to be," you might say. Give the dollar in your hand another little pull. "I don't understand that. This one seems as strong as ever."

You'll probably get a big laugh. At this point,

someone has to explain to you that a strong dollar or a weak dollar means buying power. Listen carefully, but shake your head.

"This dollar, (and here you hold up the bill in your hand) seems strong enough to me. In fact, I'll just prove it is strong."

Hold up a long pencil that you just "happen" to have handy. Ask the person who tried to explain strong and weak money to help you.

"Please hold one end of this pencil firmly against the top of this desk. I'll show you how strong this dollar bill is."

Place the pencil so that most of it sticks out over the edge of the desk or table. Have your helper push down hard on the other end of the pencil.

Raise the dollar bill over your head as you hold it between your thumb and the rest of your fingers. Then, with one fast motion, bring that hand down hard. To everyone's surprise (except yours) the pencil breaks!

"See, I told you this dollar was strong." It is now your turn to look pleased and even smile a little.

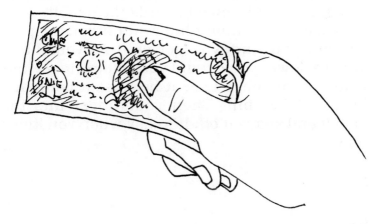

When the onlookers want to try this themselves you might suggest, "Let's use a different dollar bill. We already know this one is a strong dollar."

Unless others know the trick, no matter what bills they use the pencil won't break. Someone will eventually demand to try your bill.

When that happens, just shrug and lend them your dollar bill. Of course, this bill won't break the pencil either.

Now you can look puzzled and ask, "Do you suppose my strong dollar got weak?" Pick it up and sure enough, you can still break the pencil with it.

"Nope. My dollar is still strong."

How long you want to insist your dollar is strong is up to you. You can use other dollar bills and they will suddenly become "strong" in your hands.

When you run short of pencils to break, you may want to explain the trick. Or you may suddenly find your dollar is "weak" and no longer breaks pencils! It's up to you.

The trick is so simple it's hard to discover. It depends on the quick swing you make as you bring the dollar down towards the pencil.

Of course, the dollar bill won't break the pencil—but your index finger will! As your hand sweeps down, you extend your index finger, but your victim doesn't see it because it is hidden by the dollar bill. Then your finger hits the pencil and snaps it off. It's easy when you know how.

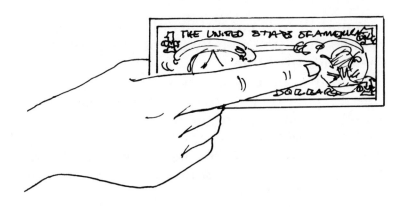

It's All
in the Wrist

Set a soft drink bottle on top of a table. Actually, any bottle will work that has a top about the size of a soft drink bottle.

Tear a strip about an inch wide from the long end of a sheet of notebook paper. Hold one end on top of the bottle.

Stack 4 coins on the strip of paper over the bottle. Make certain the larger coins are on the bottom if there is a difference in sizes. Three coins will work just as well as 4.

Next, suggest that it is easy to pull the paper out from under the coins without spilling the coins.

Be sure to add, "Don't touch the coins or the bottle."

25

No matter how careful people are when they try this, the coins usually fall off the paper and bottle onto the table.

When everyone is pretty certain it can't be done it's your chance to come to the rescue.

Hold the loose end of the paper strip firmly in one hand. Bring the other hand down as fast as possible at about the middle of the paper strip.

The sudden jerk will whip the paper out from under the coins. They will stay on top of the bottle. You will still be holding the paper strip by one end.

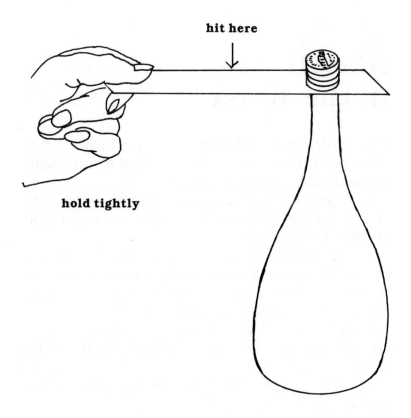

CARDS AND DICE CAN BE TRICKY

Pick a Card

You don't need to practise this card trick more than once or twice. It's easy to do; it works every time; and it fools most people time and time again.

Hand your victim a deck of cards and say something like, "Pick a card, and don't let me see the card you pick. Just make sure you look at it long enough so that you remember which card it is. While you're looking at it, your brain waves will tell me which card it is."

This remark will probably invite some laughs and rude remarks, but don't pay any attention. Your time is coming.

"Now," you instruct your victim, "put the card you chose on top of the deck."

When this is done, you continue, "Now cut the deck once."

This buries the chosen card somewhere in the middle of the deck.

At this point, you pick up the deck of cards and begin taking the cards off and turning them over one at a time. When you reach the proper card you hesitate, pretend to think, then say, "This is the card you chose."

Of course, you have picked the proper card and your victim wonders how. Offer to do it again. It works every time.

What makes this such a good trick is that it's so simple most people can't figure it out. They try to find a difficult answer instead of watching what you do.

What you must do always is see what card is on the very *bottom* of the deck. It is easy to do this when you hand the deck to your victim.

When the victim chooses a card, that card goes on *top* of the deck.

When the deck is cut, the bottom stack of cards goes on top. This puts the bottom card right on top of the card your victim picked.

So when you start sorting through the deck, the bottom card—which you already recognize—comes right before the chosen card. It's as easy as that!

For variety, you may want to go past the correct card for a few cards and then return to it. In such a case, you might say, "Wait. Something is wrong here. Your brain waves are telling me I've gone too far." Then slowly go back through the cards and find the proper one.

Since you are the star of this act, it's up to you how much of a show you want to put on. It is not magic but most people can't ever figure out how the trick works.

Dice-Reading Trick

Hand a friend 4 dice (they don't have to be the same size or color). Tell your friend to look at the dice carefully; then stack them, one die on top of the other. (One is a die; 2 or more are dice, by the way.)

You say: "I will turn my back while you stack the 4 dice. Then, when I turn around, I am going to look very closely at the one on top. I will not touch any of them.

"Using just the power of my mind I can see through the dice in the stack. This will allow me to tell you the total number of spots on the sides of the dice that are hidden below."

Even if you are using clear dice, this is obviously impossible. There is no way you could see the spots on the 7 hidden sides of all 4 dice.

Turn around and let your friend go to work. When it's time to do your mind reading you may want to make a production out of it. Peer closely. Look puzzled. Chant magic words. Do whatever makes the trick more dramatic. Then give the correct answer.

Here's how it works. Just subtract the number of spots on top from 28. The difference will be the total of the spots on the 7 hidden sides (or faces) of the dice in the stack.

If the top side has 3 spots, for example, 7 hidden sides total 25. If a 5 is showing, the hidden sides total 23, and so on.

Why does that always work? Because the opposite sides of a die always add up to 7. Check one just to make sure. Six is opposite one. Five is opposite 2, and 3 and 4 are opposite each other.

Knowing this, you see how this mind reading—or dice reading—trick works: The top and bottom face of each die must add up to 7. Four times 7 equals 28. Subtract the value of the top face from 28 and you have the total for the 7 hidden faces.

Use a little showmanship; don't give the answer too quickly, and you can probably get away with this trick many times.

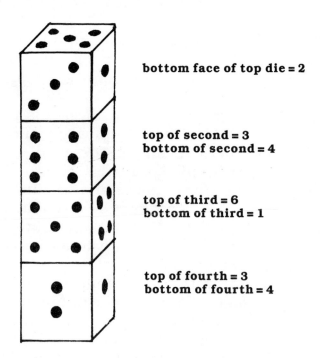

bottom face of top die = 2

top of second = 3
bottom of second = 4

top of third = 6
bottom of third = 1

top of fourth = 3
bottom of fourth = 4

In this example, subtract 5 from 28 and the total of the 7 hidden faces has to be 23.

Make several stacks of dice and check out this trick. Then amaze your friends with your skill.

Drop Shot

The trick that makes this stunt work is knowing how to do it.

Place a saucepan or kettle on the floor. Or, if you prefer, turn a hat or cap upside down on the floor.

Take 10 cards from a deck. Make the following challenge.

"I will hand you these cards one at a time. Hold the card at waist level above the pan. Drop it into the pan. You drop 10 cards. Then I will drop 10. The one who gets the most cards into the pan wins."

That's all there is to it—a simple test of skill. (Naturally, there is a trick to it.)

When you hand your opponent the cards, make sure the edges are angled down. Most likely your friend will drop the cards that way.

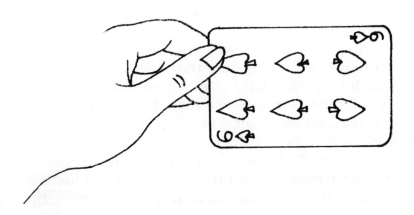

Drop a few cards edge down and see what happens as they fall.

Now hold a card so that the *flat* side is down. Hold it by both edges and let go of it so that it falls with the flat side down.

Do this a few times and you'll see the difference. Cards dropped like this are more likely to fall nearly straight down. Cards dropped with an edge down tend to flutter off to one side before reaching the floor.

Just be sure your opponent goes first. You should win this contest without any problems.

Tricky Dice Totals

As you begin this trick take a minute to tell your friends how you just happened to learn you had magic powers. Quite by accident, you discovered you could read the minds of people who rolled dice.

Naturally, no one will believe you. They will probably even tell you that they don't think much of such a wild tale. All you can do when that happens is to prove that they are wrong.

Have someone roll 2 dice without letting you see the numbers rolled.

You say: "Add the 2 numbers that are showing. Remember that total, but don't tell me."

Once this is done, have him or her pick up *one* of the dice.

"Read the number on the back and add it to the total you just got. *Do not* pick up the other die," you continue.

"One more time, roll the die you picked up. Add the number that comes up to the total and think very hard about that total number. Do not touch either of the dice again."

When your helper has this final total in mind, it is time for you to take a look at the 2 dice. You glance at them and instantly tell anyone who is interested what the total number is that your helper has in mind.

This trick seems so easy that it really upsets people who see it. Time and time again, you have the proper total yet no one can see how you do it—which, of course, is what makes it such a great trick.

Here is how it works: When you look at the 2 dice, you see the original number on one of them. The other has the number from its second roll showing.

Add these 2 numbers together. Add 7 to that number. The result is the total your helper has in mind.

Let's do a quick example: The dice are rolled. One shows 3, the other shows 5. Three plus 5 equal 8.

Your helper picks up the 3 which has a 4 on the reverse side. Four added to 8 brings the total to 12.

That die is rolled again and comes up 2. Twelve and 2 are 14. This is the grand total.

When you glance at the dice you see the original 5 and the new 2. You add 5 and 2 to get 7. Then you add 7 more and arrive at 14. Neat trick, did I hear you say?

Run through this with dice a few times before you do it in public. Just be sure you choose a helper or friend or victim who can add numbers. If that person makes mistakes in addition, your trick will go sour. You won't have to read minds to know what people think when your trick backfires!

The Standing Card

A playing card or a 3×5-inch file card can be made to stand on edge. All it takes is a little know-how.

Pretend to work hard at making the card stand on edge—any edge. Of course, it keeps falling over.

Insist that you saw someone do this trick. "I won't give up until I make this card stand," you say.

Just as soon as anyone tells you that this trick is impossible to do, you have the signal to perform.

Hold the card in the palm of one hand. Cup your fingers just slightly. This puts a curve into the card. Rub the curve into the card with the fingers of your other hand. Within a few seconds the card will have a slight curve in itself. It won't be flat anymore.

Now stand the card with one of the curved edges on the table. It will stand up just the way you said it would.

"There. I knew it would stand by itself!" you announce.

Don't expect people to congratulate you. It's hard to say nice things when you're grinding your teeth!

The Next Card Is Yours

Just about everyone enjoys being asked to pick a card from a pack and then trying to hide it so that it cannot be identified. This is one time when the victim may enjoy the trick even more than you do.

For this stunt, you need a deck of cards with a picture on the back. *Don't* use cards with a back design that looks the same upside down or right side up. A picture of a dog or a boat (or anything that's different when turned around) is what you need.

Before showing this trick to anyone, go through the deck and make sure all the backs are turned the same way. Hold the deck out to your victim. You may want to fan the cards when you do this.

You say, "Pick one card. Do not let go of it. Memorize that card."

While the victim is intent upon that one card, turn the deck in your hand. If you turn the deck casually, your victim will never notice.

35

"Slip the card into the deck," you say, continuing the trick.

(By now, the trick is already obvious to you. All the cards are now pointing one way *except* for the chosen card.) Cut the deck 3 or 4 times to conceal the chosen card. Be absolutely certain you don't turn part of the deck yourself.

"Now to locate your card," you can say confidently.

Leave the deck with the backs of the cards facing up. Slowly turn over the cards, one at a time. The chosen card will be easy to spot. It will be the one whose back faces the wrong way.

Don't react until you see the card's face, of course. When this card's face appears you can make a little production out of it.

"Is this the one?" Hesitate and look puzzled. You may even start to turn over another card. Then go back, shake your head and say, "This is the one, isn't it."

If you repeat this trick, naturally, you must turn the card so that it again points in the same direction as the rest of the deck.

If you want to be really tricky about this, here's an idea: When you locate the proper card, memorize its face, but don't say anything. Instead, continue turning over a few more cards. Then begin to look bothered. Turn over one more card. Smile and look pleased.

"The next card I pick up is your card," you can tell your victim.

No way! The chosen card was turned up several cards back. Your victim is pretty certain you've tricked yourself and will probably say something like, "I'll bet you are wrong."

After your victim lets you know how wrong you are, go back through the cards and pick up the right one. Then watch your victim, who has just been tricked—but good!

The Tattletale Reversed Card

When you want to really confuse others with your trickery, show them this card trick.

Place 5 or 6 cards on the table. Build up to your trick like this.

You say "In just a minute, I am going to turn my back. While my back is turned, I want you to reverse one of these cards. Put it back in its exact place. Then I will turn around and be able to tell you which card you reversed."

Naturally, you can do exactly what you claim to do. Study the cards shown to see how this trick works.

Take a good look at the three of hearts; 2 of the hearts point downwards and only one

points upwards. The nine of spades has 5 spades pointing upwards and only 4 pointing downwards. The same is true for the six of hearts and five of hearts.

Can you now see how the trick works? When one of these cards is reversed, there will be a difference in the way the spots or markings appear to you. Reverse the three of hearts, and suddenly 2 hearts point upwards instead of downwards.

Flip through a deck of cards. You will find a number of cards that are different when they are reversed. Choose 5 or 6 of these different cards and get ready to show your trick.

Beware of sevens and aces! Sevens and aces (except for the ace of diamonds) can be used for this trick, but they are too obvious and would give the trick away. Take a look at them yourself to see why.

You may want to add a little hocus-pocus with this trick. "Cards have a way of telling people they have been touched," you may tell the person you want to trick. "They give off heat from your hand. No matter how lightly you touch a card, just the contact changes that card. I can feel that when I run my hand over the cards."

This is utter nonsense and most people know it. Some victims will touch all the cards in an effort to throw you off, however.

After a card is reversed, you can tell at a glance which one was turned. In the above illustration, all 4 cards have the greatest number of one-way markings at the top of the card. It's simple to identify the one that is reversed.

To really convince people how tricky you can

be, allow your victim to reverse more than one card or even not to reverse any cards.

"I will know. The cards always tell me," you can boast, which is true, isn't it?

The Tattletale Chosen Card

Once you have The Tattletale Reversed Card stunt under control, try this one.

Sort through a deck of cards and pull out *all* the cards that change their appearance when they are reversed. This includes the sevens and aces, as well as most threes, fives, sixes, and nines.

If some tricky person asks why there aren't any diamonds, you can show the seven and, hopefully, end the questions. Or, you can say,

"I don't like diamonds. They make me think of mortgage payments and that sort of thing." You can come up with some good reason.

Set up the cards you have chosen so that they all "point" in the same direction. Here's an example:

"Pick a card," you instruct your opponent. "Memorize it."

While the other person's attention is on the card he or she just picked, you reverse the deck. (Sounds like the trick, "The Next Card Is Yours," doesn't it?)

When the chosen card is slipped back into the deck, it will "point" in the opposite direction from the others in the pack.

Make a show of turning the cards, face up, one at a time. It won't be hard to spot the chosen card. Pull it out and hand it over. As you do, it's the most natural thing in the world to give it a half turn while you offer it to the other person. This, of course, has it "pointing" the same way as the other cards. Just make sure it stays this way when it's returned to the pack.

This trick borrows ideas from two other tricks and comes out with an entirely new version. It illustrates how really clever you can become when learning the game.

40

Mind-Reading Dice

Hand your victim 3 dice. It doesn't matter whether they match or not. And say something, for example:

"If you can do some fourth-grade math, I can make these dice into mind-reading dice."

Naturally, your victim can do fourth-grade math. What sort of question is that?

"Just to prove I can do a mind-reading trick with these dice I want you to roll them. Be sure to keep them out of my sight. But this is very important. Don't touch them after they stop rolling. If you touch them you'll ruin the trick."

This is all nonsense. But the dice roller doesn't know that. The warning about not touching the dice is what is called "misdirection." It makes your victim wonder what would happen if he or she did touch the dice instead of thinking about how the trick works.

Once the dice are rolled, give these instructions.

"Double the number of spots showing on the die that is farthest to your left.

"Now, add 5 to the number you got when you doubled.

"Multiply this answer by 5.

"Now, add the number of spots showing on the middle die.

"Next, multiply that last answer by 10.

"Add to this last answer the number of spots on the third die.

"Finally, tell me the total you got when you added the final number."

Once you have that total number, you pretend to concentrate hard for a few seconds. Then look pleased, and tell your victim the number of spots showing on each of the 3 dice.

This is a good stunt which works over and over. The only way it can go wrong is if one of you messes up the fourth-grade math.

Here's how it works. Suppose your friend rolled the dice and they came up like this.

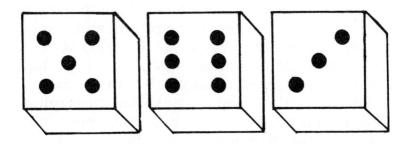

Double the spots on the left-hand die: $5 \times 2 = 10$.

Add 5: $10 + 5 = 15$.

Multiply by 5: $15 \times 5 = 75$.

Add the middle die: $75 + 6 = 81$.

Multiply by 10: $81 \times 10 = 810$.

Add 3: $810 + 3 = 813$.

Now, without telling your victim what you are doing, you must subtract 250 from the answer. $813 - 250 = 563$. The answer you got—563—gives you the top numbers of the 3 dice in order from left to right.

This is a great trick. You can do it many times without having it fail.

The Last Card

When people are showing off their best card tricks, you may want to demonstrate this nasty little fooler.

"What I am going to do," you tell your friends, "is to name the last card one of you turns over."

Give this trick all the buildup you want. Shuffle the deck a few times. Then give it to your victim and suggest, "Why don't you shuffle the deck yourself?"

Then you say, "Please cut the deck at least 4 times."

Once this is all taken care of, ask for part of the deck of cards. "Cut the deck one more time. Without looking at any of the cards give half of the deck to me. You take the other half."

When you have your cards in hand, say, "Now, go into the next room. Close the door behind you. Turn over as many cards from your part of the deck as you want. After you have turned over some or even all the cards, come back into this room. When you do I'll tell you the card that was the last one you turned over."

Who can resist the chance to prove you can't do what you say?

As soon as your friend walks into the next room and the door closes, take one card from your part of the pack. Lean that card against the closed door. When the door opens, this card will get turned over.

Sneaky, isn't it? Naturally, you can name the

last card to be turned over. You chose it when you leaned it against the door.

You Picked This Card?

People are quite used to being asked to pick a card from a deck. The trick is always that the magician, or whoever, will then discover that card.

This trick is really annoying.

Tell your victim, "Pick a card. Any card. Don't let me see it. Memorize it. Put it back into the pack. Then shuffle the pack. Cut it as many times as you wish."

When this is done, ask for the cards. Announce, "I will hand you the card you picked."

All you have to do is return the cards to your victim.

"Here. The card you picked is in here. I just handed you the card you picked."

You can expect some nasty remarks when the victim realizes you have played one more trick. If those things bothered you, you wouldn't be playing more sneaky tricks.

If you want to make this trick last longer, hand your victim one card at a time. Each time, ask, "Is this the card?"

You will eventually reach the correct card. When that happens, you might look pleased with yourself and say, "See, I told you I'd hand you the card you picked."

Don't expect much praise, especially if you went through most of the deck to reach the chosen card.

TRICKS WITH STRINGS AND THINGS

Don't Lose Your Head

Start with a piece of string about 3 feet long. Tie the 2 ends together to make the string into a loop.

Put the string around your neck with the 2 loops hanging in front of you. Put one thumb through each of the loops and pull the string tight (not tight enough to strangle yourself—that would ruin the trick).

Move your hands close together. As you do so, extend the index finger of one hand. With this index finger reach over and hook the loop held by the other hand. Keep the string tight all this time.

If you have used the right index finger, that right finger is now sharing the loop with your left thumb.

At this point, say something stunning, such as, "I am going to pull this string through my neck." Or, to be more dramatic you can say, "I'm going to cut off my head."

As you say this, slip your *right* thumb out of the loop. At the same time, quickly pull your right index finger and your left thumb in opposite directions. Be sure to keep the string tight.

Almost by magic the string seems to slice through your neck! Of course, it just slides *around* your neck as your right index finger and left thumb separate.

Magicians call this trick an illusion. Most people call it sneaky. No matter what you call it, this one always surprises people the first time they see it.

Tying a Tricky Knot

For this trick, you need a piece of cord or a string about 3 feet long. You can also use a scarf or a large handkerchief instead of the string.

Hold up the cord or whatever, so that one end is in your right hand and the other is in your left.

Announce, "I can tie a knot in this piece of cord."

That's not exactly the news story of the year, but it will let your victims know you have another trick for them.

"I can tie a knot in this cord *without* letting go of either end."

This boast is something else! It's clearly impossible. Or is it?

Let your audience experiment before you begin. If someone else knows the trick, you can compliment that person and say, "See, I told you it could be done."

But if everyone else fails you can come to their rescue. Just fold your arms. Then take hold of one end of the cord in each hand. (It is trickier to get hold of the 2 ends with your arms folded than it is to do the trick!)

To tie the knot, just unfold your arms while holding onto the ends of the cord. A knot will appear in the middle of the cord.

Your victims will undoubtedly say, "Oh, that's easy."

Just remind them it was *you* who showed them how.

A Knotty Problem

Tying a knot in the middle of a shoelace or piece of cord is not much of a trick. But tying a knot using only one hand makes it much more interesting.

Hold a fairly long shoelace or piece of cord in your hand. Work up to this trick with a few well-chosen words, such as:

"When you are as skillful and as talented as I am, it's easy to do things other people find nearly impossible."

After an opening like that who can resist taking a potshot at you?

You continue, "Just using one hand I can tie a knot in this shoelace. I won't let the lace touch the rest of my body. I won't have to cheat by letting the lace touch anything besides my hand."

Your victim will take a look at the lace and decide the task can't be all that difficult. After all, you say you can do it. Why can't anyone?

It is not impossible to tie the necessary knot. It is just difficult—unless you do it properly. That, of course, is the trick.

Let your victims work on this trick for a few minutes. Don't be surprised if someone manages to get a knot into the lace. It can be done. Just don't allow the lace to touch anything but the player's hand and fingers.

If someone gets the knot into place, be quick to congratulate that person. Then add, "Of course, I can do it in less than 5 seconds!" This is probably a lot quicker than the time it takes anyone else to tie the knot.

When the time comes to put up or shut up, be ready to amaze and dazzle. If you practise this trick a few times, you'll be able to do it quickly enough so that the people watching *still* won't be able to tie the knot, even though they just saw it done!

Hang the shoelace or cord over your thumb

as shown below. Let the end next to your palm hang down lower than the other end.

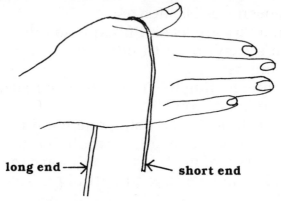

long end ⟶ ⟵ short end

First, hook the long side of the cord with your ring finger so that it is now between your middle finger and your ring finger. It looks like this.

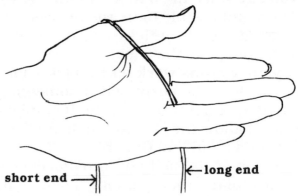

short end ⟶ ⟵ long end

Second, turn your hand so that your palm is now facing the floor. The back of your hand is now on top.

Third, as you turn your hand palm down the cord swings just a bit. Grab the *short* end of the cord between your thumb and forefinger.

Fourth, tip your hand downwards. The loop on the back of your hand will slide off your fingers. Hold onto the short end of the cord and jerk your hand upwards.

Believe it or not, that's all there is to it. There you are, holding the end of the cord between your thumb and forefinger. A knot has been made somewhere near the middle of the shoelace or cord.

Though it may be difficult, try to look modest as you show your victims how quickly you tied the knot using only your wits and one hand.

The Famous Ring-Off-the-String Trick

This trick is not magic, though many magicians use it to amaze their audiences. It is absolutely, positively, *guaranteed* to surprise your victim. You'll need string and a ring.

Begin with a piece of string about 3 feet long. Tie the ends together. Now you have a loop of string. Have your victim (or helper, or whoever) hold up both index fingers.

Slip one end of the loop over one index finger. Run the rest of the string through the middle of the ring. Loop the other end of the string over your friend's other index finger.

"Now," you announce, "here is what I am going to do. I am going to remove the ring from the string. The string won't be cut or untied. Neither will it be slipped from either index finger."

It doesn't take a whole lot of thinking to re-alize that this seems impossible. Of course it is not. Otherwise, how could you make this trick work?

With your left hand take hold of the side of the string farther from you. Pull it *over* the nearer part of the string and hold onto it.

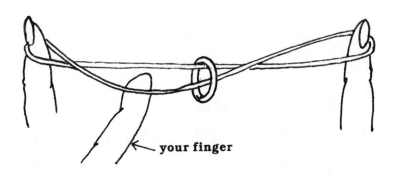

← your finger

Next, reach *under* the part of the string you are holding with your left hand. Take hold of the far string. Pull it towards you. Make certain the ring is to your right and out of the way.

As you pull on the string with your right hand you will form a loop. The person holding the string will have to move both hands a little closer together to give you the slack you need to make the loop.

Hook this loop over the holder's finger. Since you are facing the person holding the string, this is to *your left*, but to the other person's right.

Once this loop is hooked over the holder's in-dex finger let go of it with your right hand. *Do not* let go of the string your left hand is still holding.

52

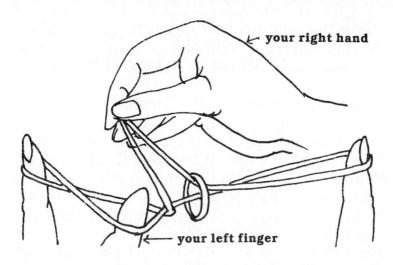

your right hand

your left finger

Now it is time to work to *your right* of the ring. Reach over the string nearer to you. Take hold of the farther string with your right hand. Don't let go with your left hand or you'll have to start all over again.

With your right hand, gently pull one more loop in the string. Your holder will have to let you have enough string to work with by moving both hands closer together again.

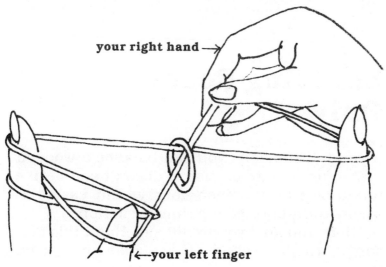

your right hand →

←your left finger

Now, for the moment of truth! Take hold of the ring with your right hand. Let go of the loop of string you have held for so long with your left hand.

Maybe you want to say, "Brace yourself," to the string holder. Then very, very slowly begin to pull on the ring. You may need to wiggle the ring up and down a bit because those loops of string need to slip around the holder's finger.

As the strings slip and you keep pulling gently on the ring, a strange thing happens. To everyone's surprise (maybe even to yours unless you've done this trick many times) the ring is suddenly off the string.

There you are holding the ring in your right hand. The string never left the holder's fingers—yet it is off the string!

Practise this one until you get the technique smooth and perfect. It will help build your reputation as a really tricky character.

Standing Room Only

If you tell someone you can balance a wooden match on a plate or dish it doesn't sound like much of a trick. When your victim yawns or seems unimpressed it's time for action.

"Here you go," you might say. Hand this person a wooden match and a dish or saucer.

"Why don't you make this match stand up on the dish?"

Give your unfortunate friend time enough to become really frustrated before showing how the trick works.

Whether you get pretty tricky or not yourself is entirely up to you. If you want to be tricky, hold the end of the match between your lips as you pretend to do something with the plate. (Not the head of the match, naturally.)

What you are doing is getting the end of the match good and damp. Or you may be able to wet your finger or thumb and use that moisture to dampen the match.

Once the end of the match is good and damp, press it down hard onto the plate. Hold it in place for a few seconds while pressing down good and hard.

Think of something confusing to say to cover the fact that you are pressing down so hard on the damp match fibres.

"Due to the earth's movement through space I have to hold the match long enough for it to adjust to its changed position," is a possible statement.

Or you can say, "I am realigning the match's molecules."

When you let go of the match it *should* stand upright. If it topples, wet the end and start over.

The best part of this trick is the reaction you get when people see you do what they couldn't do. Whether or not you want to conceal the fact that you dampened the end of the match is entirely up to you.

Potato Pickup

A medium-sized potato or an apple and 2 plastic drinking straws are all you need for this quick trick.

A good way to begin is to say, " I can never figure out how people pick up their food with chopsticks." "How could you pick up this potato (or apple) with these?" By "these," you mean the plastic straws, of course.

After someone tells you it is impossible to pick up a whole potato with chopsticks or that straws are not chopsticks, it is time to set up your victims.

Insist that you saw someone pick up a potato with chopsticks made from drinking straws. "If he can do it, you should be able to," you may add.

Encourage your victims to at least make the attempt to do the trick. If your friends are determined enough, they will probably be able to lift the potato or apple between the ends of the straws by holding the straws right down at the bottom.

"That's the way." Compliment a job well done. Then say, "But now I remember. The person I saw did it with only one straw."

This is impossible and someone will tell you it is. But a good trickster never accepts defeat, and it's time for you to make your play.

Take the straw in your hand. Wrap your 4 fingers around it and place your thumb tightly over the open end at the top.

Make sure your thumb stays tightly over the

opening. Plunge the straw down hard and fast into the potato or apple. It will stick into the potato without bending or breaking the straw.

Lift the potato by the straw and say, "I told you I could do it."

What happens is that your thumb traps the air inside the straw. When you stab the potato, this trapped air compresses and keeps the straw straight.

Try this one before doing it in public. Here's a hint. Apples are sometimes easier to stab than are potatoes.

Getting a Handle on It

This is a good follow-up stunt to use after you pick up a potato or an apple with a straw. In fact, you can use the same straw.

By the way, plastic bottles work best, especially the kinds with a "shoulder," such as the one shown here. Beware of the large soft drink bottles; they usually won't work.

Waving the straw like a pointer, touch a bottle with it. "I can pick up that bottle with this straw. And I won't even touch the bottle. All I'll do is hold onto the straw," you announce.

Let the others give it a try just so that they can see how unlikely it is that you can pull this one off. The plastic straw isn't strong enough to lift the bottle, even if the bottle could be balanced on it.

When it is time for you to shine, all you need do is bend the straw about a third of the way from the bottom. Poke the doubled end through the neck of the bottle. Once the bent part is inside the bottle it will try to unfold.

At this point, it looks something like this.

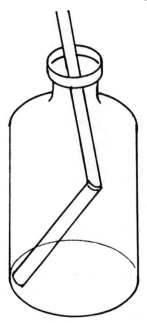

Tip the straw so that the main part is pressed against one side of the bottle. The bent end *must* touch the other side and be pointing more upwards than to the side.

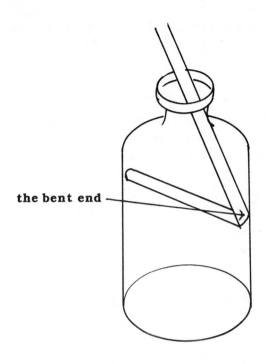

the bent end

Lift carefully, and up comes the bottle. You can even raise a bottle which is partly full of water, if you choose your bottle correctly.

Experiment first. Otherwise, you may become your own victim.

Tricky Ice Cube Pickup

It is not difficult to pick up an ice cube. Most of us do it every day. If you tell someone you can pick up an ice cube, the best you can expect is a laugh or a shake of the head.

But tell that same person you can pick up an ice cube with a short piece of string and you'll see some interest.

"I can pick up an ice cube with this piece of string. I won't touch the ice cube with my fingers in any way. All I have to do is to place my tricky string in my hand, and the string will lift the ice cube," you can predict.

Your victim will probably demand to see this tricky piece of string. Since the string is really just a common ordinary piece of string, there is nothing to see.

Offer to let your victim use your tricky string.

"What if I tie a loop in this string?" he or she may ask first.

I don't have to tie a loop in the string," you reply. "Anyone can do it that way."

Eventually, most people will give up after trying to pick up the melting ice cube without success. A lucky individual may manage to wind the string around the cube and lift it, but this is a clumsy way of doing things.

When it is time for you to show your stuff, get a fresh ice cube from the freezer. Wet the end of your string. Drop the wet end onto the ice cube. Sprinkle a bit of salt onto the wet end of the string and the surrounding ice.

Wait a few seconds; then gently lift the string. The ice cube should come right up. Just to be on the safe side, practise this a couple of times before you perform this trick. You don't have to use a fresh ice cube, but since the one from the freezer will be colder than the one your victim has been messing with, it works better.

What's So Tricky About That?

When is a trick not a trick? That's a good question. This little stunt with a rubber band may give us the answer.

Stick out your index finger. Slip one end of a rubber band over the end of your finger. Then turn the bottom of the rubber band one-half turn to the *right*. It forms a figure eight.

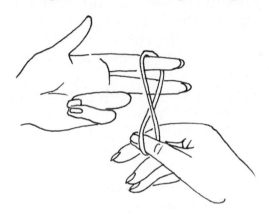

Next, bring the bottom of the figure eight down under your middle finger. Then pull it up and hook it onto the tip of your index finger. Now your not-so-tricky trick is set up and ready to go.

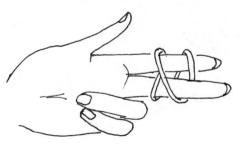

Pull the thumb down towards the tip of your index finger. Wiggle your middle finger a few times. Out of nowhere and without warning, the rubber band will fly off your hand and out into space!

At this point, expect your victim to be unimpressed and say something, such as, "Big deal" or, "So what?"

Hand over the rubber band and tell this person, "Your turn."

Then the real fun begins. Even though people watch you set this one up, very few can do it on their own the first time they try the stunt. They either turn the rubber band in the wrong direction or get their middle finger into the loop.

Be sure to try this one alone for a few times. Learn to work the stunt quickly. Find just the right length of rubber band for your fingers. Then practise aiming the rubber band when it snaps off your fingers.

This stunt is not terribly complicated. But it will make you shine in the limelight for a few minutes.

SURPRISES AND FOOLERS

Huff and Puff

Turn an empty soda bottle on its side. Crush a small piece of paper into a tight wad.

Choose a victim who is a real braggart and deserves to be squelched. Ask him or her to watch what you do.

"Look closely," you say, as you begin. "I am putting this wad of paper right here in the open end of the bottle."

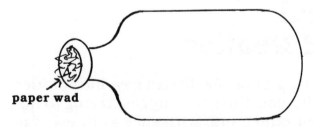

paper wad

You continue, "What I want you to do is to blow the paper into the bottle with only one breath of air. Now, just to be fair, I need to warn you of something. This is very difficult. Most people just can't blow hard enough to do it.

"Get a deep breath. Then *blow really hard.* Just remember you only get one try, so make that first blast of air do the trick."

By now, you have your victim convinced it is necessary to blow for all he or she is worth. What happens when the victim blows hard is a real surprise.

The paper wad does not go into the bottle. It does just the opposite. It flies out into the face of the huffer and puffer. The harder he or she blows, the faster the paper wad shoots out of the bottle.

This trick depends upon a hard blast of air. That is why you need to stress how hard the victim must blow. A tiny little dribble of air may allow the paper wad to slip into the bottle.

This trick really takes the wind out of a person's sails.

A Real Mind Reader

Start a discussion of ESP and psychic abilities. Eventually, someone will suggest trying to find someone in the group with such abilities. If no one makes the suggestion, you have to. Without a "psychic," there is no trick.

Have the chosen person leave the group and

go into another room. Let the group decide on one object. Everyone will think about that object. When the person returns to the room he or she will try to pick up thought waves and name the object.

Of course, it's just luck if the chosen object is named quickly. (Just luck, that is, unless someone does have psychic ability!)

Let 2 or 3 people try their luck with this game. Then send your victim out for a turn. Now, for the trick. Actually this is a reverse trick, as you will soon see.

Tell the others, "Let's make this person think he or she really has the power to read minds. No matter what the first guess is, we'll all look surprised and say that's what we were thinking about."

Naturally, the victim is surprised and pleased. Suggest a second attempt.

This time, tell the group it will be the second thing named.

The next time, make it the third thing named. Then go back to saying it is the first guess the victim makes.

By picking the second or third guess, victims don't catch on that they are being taken for a ride.

If the victim is a nice person you might eventually explain the trick. If not, you may decide not to, then when your victim brags about this newly discovered ability to others and is asked for a demonstration, the trick will be twice as good!

More Difficult than It Looks

Choose your opponent carefully for this trick. It is a good one, because it's more difficult than it seems to be at first. Some people may be strong enough to defeat you.

When an opponent does get the better of you, always remember to be gracious and congratulate that individual. After all, it pays to be polite to people who are stronger than you.

To set this trick up, stand straight. Put the palm of your hand on the top of your head. You may even pretend your hand is stuck there, if you want to.

"Can you help me lift my hand off my head?" you ask. "Just push up on my forearm, please."

Naturally, you will push down as hard as you can. The trick comes when someone tries to lift up on your forearm to remove your hand.

It is much harder than you'd expect it to be.

To increase your odds, stand so that your opponent is lifting with an outstretched arm. Don't let anyone get under your arm and push straight up.

The Coin Under the Cup

Some tricks work every time, others most of the time. This excellent trick *almost always* works. Once in a while, though, a victim may turn the tables and outsmart you.

You need 2 coins that are alike: 2 pennies or 2 quarters or whatever. Place one coin on top of the table. Keep the other in your pocket.

Hand your victim a cup. Say, "Please put the cup upside down over the coin."

When this is done, ask whether the victim is certain the coin is still under the cup.

Of course he or she is certain.

"Just to make sure do you want to check?" you ask.

It does not matter whether the victim checks or not. The important part is to get your victim used to picking up the cup.

When the victim says the coin is still under the cup, it's time for some stagecraft.

"I can remove that coin without moving the cup," you announce grandly.

Ask the victim or someone else to put a bowl or a pan over the cup.

Then have someone put a towel over the bowl or pan. This stacking of items can go on as long as you want to keep putting things over the coin.

Eventually, it is time to perform. Make a few "magic" motions over the pile of coverings. You can mutter a few "magic" words.

Then remove the top item from the pile. Make

another motion. Utter a few words. Take away the next covering.

Play out this performance with style. Finally, you will get down to the cup. At this point, tap the bottom of the cup with your index finger. This keeps everyone looking at the cup.

Take the second coin from your pocket without letting anyone know what you are doing. Keep it hidden in your hand.

After tapping the cup a few times, step back. Hold both hands together over your head.

"Without moving the cup, I have recovered the coin."

When asked to prove this, you show the coin you took from your pocket. Most victims will immediately lift the cup to check.

When that happens, quickly grab the coin from under the cup.

Give everyone your best smile. "See? I took the coin from under the cup but did not have to remove the cup."

Sure, this is a dirty trick. But being a trickster can be a dirty job.

The Stubborn Card

Many people take it personally when they cannot do something. When this happens, they try harder and harder to do it. Maybe they have to prove that they are stronger or smarter than the trick that fooled them.

Here is just the trick for the person who can't stand being outdone by even a card or a string.

A piece of file card—about 2 inches long by 3 inches wide—is great for this trick. Any piece of stiff paper will work, however. It doesn't have to be exactly 2 by 3, but cut it to approximately that size.

Bend down each of the long sides about one-quarter of an inch. When you're finished, the card should look like this:

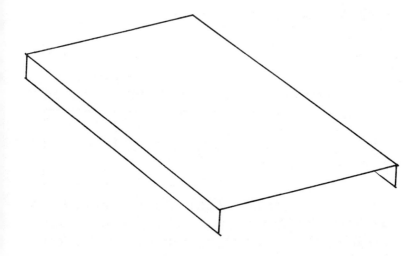

Set the card on a table or desk. (The slicker the surface, the better.)

"Just blow hard under that card, hard enough to turn it over," you command. Then stand back and watch frustration set in.

The card slips and skids around, but is practically impossible to blow over.

Just about the only way to blow the card over is not the obvious way. I've seen some people make it turn over when they blow down on the table several inches *in front* of the card. Others never can make the card turn over no matter where they blow.

Do set one ground rule to begin with. "If you blow the card off the table, you lose." This keeps you from ending up on the wrong end of a good trick.

For Squares Only

Puzzles are fun, especially puzzles with a trick to them. The trick to solving this puzzle is for you to visualize squares differently—to think of squares in a manner other than ⬜ .

Tell your victim: "I can make 3 squares exactly the same size using only 8 lines. Four of these lines are exactly 2 inches long. The other 4 lines are exactly 1 inch long."

Just to be helpful, on a piece of paper, you can draw the lines you'll be using.

This puzzle doesn't seem difficult until people actually try to do it. It's hard for most people to change their ideas of a square!

When the time comes to prove that you're still the trickiest character around, draw the 3 squares like this:

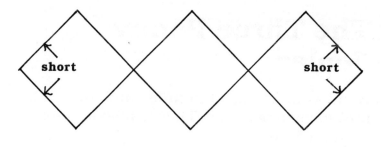

Fun *and* clever, isn't it?

WORDS ARE TRICKY— BUT SO ARE NUMBERS

The Three-Penny Fooler

Hand your victim 3 pennies and say, "These are special pennies. They can communicate with my mind."

(Should anyone be rude enough to remark that your mind is only worth 3 cents, just ignore it. Remember, they laughed at Columbus.)

Then you give a very important command.

"Without letting me see, put some pennies in your right hand and the rest in your left."

When this is done, continue giving directions. "Mentally multiply the number of pennies in your right hand by 3."

Pause while he or she multiplies. Then go on, "Now multiply the number of pennies in your left hand by 4."

"Add the 2 products together and tell me the total," you say next.

When you hear the sum of the 2 numbers, you can tell at once which hand is holding the *odd number* of pennies. Tell your victim.

Here's how the trick works.

$$
\begin{array}{cc}
\text{L} & \text{R} \\
4 & 3 \\
\times 2 & \times 1 \\
\hline
8 & 3
\end{array}
$$

$$
\begin{array}{r}
8 \\
+\ 3 \\
\hline
11 \text{ (odd)}
\end{array}
$$

Assume the right hand holds one penny. Three times one equals 3. The 2 pennies in the left hand are multiplied by 4. The product is 8. Three plus 8 are 11.

Eleven is an *odd* number. Therefore, the right hand holds the odd number of pennies.

To make this trick seem even trickier than it is, change the multipliers the next time you give directions. Have your opponents multiply the number of pennies in their right hand by 5. Then ask them to multiply the pennies in the left hand by 2.

$$
\begin{array}{cc}
\text{L} & \text{R} \\
2 & 5 \\
\times 2 & \times 1 \\
\hline
4 & 5
\end{array}
$$

$$
\begin{array}{r}
4 \\
+5 \\
\hline
9 \text{ (odd)}
\end{array}
$$

L	R
4	7
$\times 0$	$\times 3$
0	21

21 (odd)

The thing to remember is always to use an *odd* number to multiply the pennies in the right hand. Use an *even* multiplier for the left hand.

If the final answer is odd, you'll know that the right hand holds an odd number of coins. If the final answer is even, the odd number of coins will be in the left hand.

Try this trick with 5 or 7 or 9 pennies instead of 3. Just make sure your victim always has an *odd* number of coins. And always multiply the right hand by an odd number and the left by any even number.

What if your victim decides to put all the coins in one hand? No need to worry. Just make sure you always say, "Put *some* pennies in your right hand." Even if the left hand is empty—the trick works.

Suppose the 3 pennies in the right hand are multiplied by 7 and the empty left hand is multiplied by 4. Seven times 3 are 21. Four times zero is zero. Twenty-one plus zero equals 21, an odd number. So you know the odd number of pennies has to be in the right hand.

How Many T's?

Give this quick trick a good buildup. Tell your victims something to make them curious. "It's amazing how few people can listen to even a sentence or two. They think they're listening, but really are not. I guess some people just aren't as smart as they think they are."

Naturally, your victims will want to show that they can listen. Everyone will be ready to demonstrate intelligence.

Once you have your victims practically begging to take part in your listening test, the rest is easy.

"Listen closely to what I say," you instruct.

Then, slowly and carefully, you say: "Tommy Tucker talks too much. His teacher should tell him to stop. Now tell me how many t's are there in that?"

If your victims ask you to repeat the statement, do so. *Repeat it exactly as it is written above.* Speak slowly and clearly. Make certain you pronounce each word carefully. Give your listeners all the time they need.

You may be surprised at the answers you receive. It is true that many people don't really listen. It's also true that most people find it difficult to count the number of letters that appear in a statement.

Of course, the correct answer is 2. There are 2 t's in *that*. That's what you asked. Quite clearly you said, "Now tell me how many t's are there in *that*?"

The Never-Wrong Mind Reader

"I learned to read minds," you can begin. Before anyone tells you this is impossible, hurry on. "It was in a book. I read how to do it."

For effect you might pause and then admit, "Of course, I haven't tried it yet. But I know I can do it."

When your friends stop teasing you, it's time to do your thing. Hand a pencil and paper to one person.

"Here. Write any short message on that paper. Just don't let me see what it is."

Your victim will make sure you can't see what is being written while you pretend to think deep thoughts.

"Now fold the paper. I don't want anyone to think I saw what's on the paper," you say when the message is written.

Once the paper is folded, suggest, "Fold it again. I know I can tell what's on the paper."

When the second fold is finished, make your final request. "Just to be absolutely certain I can't see through the paper, put it on the floor. Then put your foot over it. That way there can't be any doubt."

By now, your victim is certain you've flipped your lid. Anyone who's watching is beginning either to suspect a trick or to wonder if you've lost your mind. Continue and say this with confidence:

"Now. Do you want me to tell you what is on the paper?"

(Notice that you never mention what is *writ-*

ten on the paper.? You always talk about what is *on* the paper.)

Of course, everyone wants to know what is on the paper.

"Your foot is on the paper. That's what's on the paper," you declare firmly.

You are right, of course. You have come through again, just like the winner you are!

Falling in Love Is Tricky

Start this number trick by using a little of your best showmanship. Say something like this, "I just discovered some magic numbers that tell me how many times you have been in love. To help me prove this, all you have to do is to follow my easy directions. The magic numbers will do the rest."

This is too good to turn down since most people are anxious to prove there are no such things as "magic numbers."

"Start by writing your age on a piece of paper," you direct.

"Now, multiply your age by 2."

"Add 5 to the answer you got when you multiplied," you say next.

"Now multiply that answer by 50."

When your victim has done the multiplication you say, "Subtract the number of days in a normal year from the answer you just got." (That's 365, in case you run into someone who doesn't know.)

"Here's the most important step," you announce. "Add the number of times you have been in love. Since you are less than 100 years old, you can't have been in love more than 99 times, so don't try to fool me by saying you have!"

This direction is important for you. Any number *larger* than 99 in this step will mess up the magic answer.

When the addition is finished, you say, "Now, add 115." Let your victim add the numbers.

Ask for the final answer. All it will take is a quick calculation for you to know your victim's age and also how many times he or she claims to have been in love.

Let's run through this for a person who's 12 years old and claims to have been in love 3 times.

$$
\begin{array}{r}
1. \quad 12 \\
\times \quad 2 \\
\hline
24
\end{array}
$$

$$
\begin{array}{r}
2. \quad 24 \\
+ \quad 5 \\
\hline
29
\end{array}
$$

$$
\begin{array}{r}
3. \quad 29 \\
\times \quad 50 \\
\hline
1450
\end{array}
$$

$$
\begin{array}{r}
4. \quad 1450 \\
- \quad 365 \\
\hline
1085
\end{array}
$$

$$
\begin{array}{r}
5. \quad 1085 \\
+ \quad 3 \\
\hline
1088
\end{array}
$$

$$
\begin{array}{r}
6. \quad 1088 \\
+ \quad 115 \\
\hline
1203
\end{array}
$$

age   3 times

When we look at 1203 it's easy to see the first

2 digits tell the person's age is 12. The rest of the number indicates the number of times—3.

Work this problem through a few times for different ages and different numbers of times. If you don't let anyone claim to have been in love more than 99 times, this trick is a sure winner!

Half and Half

The only trick to this little brainteaser is getting over the fact that it sounds impossible.

Tell your victim this story. (Make it longer and better, if you wish.)

"A grandmother saved her change to share with her 3 grandchildren. One day when all 3 of them visited her, she had collected some quarters to give them.

"Since she liked Janice best of all, she gave her half of all the quarters, plus half a quarter.

"She didn't like Howard quite as much, so she gave him half the quarters she had left, plus half a quarter.

"Finally she got to Tommy, who had broken her favorite vase during his last visit. Since she was still upset about his carelessness, she gave the unlucky boy half the quarters she had left, plus half a quarter."

"The grandmother didn't damage any of the coins, but she did give away all the quarters she had saved. How many quarters did she begin with? How many quarters did each grandchild receive?''

If your friends solve this one for you be sure to tell them how intelligent they are. (After all, no trick works *every* single time, does it?)

If your friends give up, it's time for you to introduce some more tricky arithmetic.

The grandmother had 7 quarters. Janice got half of 7 plus a half. Half of 7 is 3½, plus a half, equals 4. So Janice picked up 4 quarters as her share of the loot.

Howard received half of the 3 remaining quarters, plus a half. Half of 3 is 1½, plus half, makes 2. This left the grandmother with only one quarter.

Poor Tommy was certainly sorry he broke his grandmother's favorite vase. He got half of that last quarter plus half a quarter which left him with one quarter.

But when you think about it, one quarter is better than none.

Wrong-Answer Time

Lots of tricks work because the person playing the trick knows exactly what to say and when to say it. By saying the right thing at the right time, it is usually possible to keep your victim off guard. That is how this trick works.

You say, "Did you know that it is almost impossible to deliberately give wrong answers to questions?" (This is a good way to begin.)

"In fact, I just heard that a person's mind will never deliberately give 5 wrong answers in a row."

This statement is more than most people can accept. When someone says, "I can give 5 wrong answers," you have a victim. The rest is up to you.

Begin by asking, "What year were you born?"

"In 1266," is a likely (certainly incorrect) answer.

Next, you might ask, "How many ounces are in a pound?"

Your victim may reply, "Ninety."

You could begin to look a bit worried, as though you are in trouble.

"What is the sum of 6 and 7?" you ask, continuing the game.

Expect a silly answer, such as "569."

Hesitate for a second or two. Then ask, "How many questions have I asked so far?"

Unless you victim is sharper than the average bear, he or she will answer, "Three." If that happens, you have won your bet.

Your victim may see through the trick and give you a wrong answer. When that happens you have to be your most tricky.

Grin, shrug, and ask, "Why did you say what you just said?"

You may luck out and be told, "Because I had to give a wrong answer."

Of course, this answer is correct and you win. If you get another wild answer, you just struck out! Sorry about that!

Missing Money

The best tricks are the ones (like this one) that completely surprise the victim.

Tell the following story to someone you want to trick. You can make the story longer and more interesting, if you like.

Three friends decided to try out the new All-You-Can-Eat Restaurant that just opened. They ate a fantastic meal—much more than they should have eaten.

"That will be $10 each," the cashier told them when they finally finished eating.

Each one of the 3 friends paid with a $10-bill.

It was only after they had left the restaurant that the cashier realized she had overcharged them. She remembered, that night the restaurant had a special price: $25 for 3 guests.

"Quick," she exclaimed, handing the waiter five $1 bills. "Run after those 3 people and give them their refund."

The waiter ran out of the restaurant and saw the 3 friends getting into their car. He waved to attract their attention. By the time he reached the car, the waiter knew he had a problem: There was no easy way to divide $5 evenly among 3 people!

"Here," he said, panting. "The cashier overcharged you." He handed each of them a dollar bill. He kept the remaining $2 for himself.

"Thank you," one of the diners said to the

waiter. To her friends she said, "This is great. It only cost us $9 each for that wonderful meal."

The 3 friends drove away. They were happy because the meal cost them only $27 instead of $30.

The waiter was pleased because he had $2 in his pocket.

But wait! The 3 people paid $30 to begin with. With their refund, they really paid $27. The waiter has $2. Twenty-seven and 2 add up to 29. What happened to the missing dollar?

Nearly every time you tell this tricky story, "Missing Money," you will fool most (if not all) of your listeners.

The trick lies in the way you figure things at the end. To have it make sense and to find the missing dollar, look at it this way:

The cashier kept $25 dollars, the waiter kept $2. The diners got back $3. Twenty-five, plus 2 plus 3 equal 30.

Hurrah! The lost dollar has been found!

That Can't Be a Word

This catchy little trick is a good one to try on a fantastic speller or someone who reads a lot.

Begin by claiming, "I know an 8-letter word. This word used to be important, but is not heard or written much anymore. Another hint, George Washington and Ben Franklin both used it. So did your great-grandmother."

By now, you can almost hear the mental wheels beginning to turn.

You continue, "The middle 3 letters in this word are *k s t, in the beginning, and at the end.*"

Your fantastic speller is really thinking now. What 8-letter word has kst in the middle, in the beginning, and at the end?

If your victim realizes that this seems to add up to 9 (instead of 8) letters, just flash your best evil smile. Obviously, there can't be such a word.

Most people give up pretty quickly.

"The word is inkstand," you announce to the quitter. "It has "kst" in the middle, "in" is the beginning. Of course, "and" is at the end."

in kst and

This is not exactly the way you described the word, but what you said was true enough. A little misdirection makes lots of tricks work. This is one of them.

Lucky
Number Seven

"Seven is my lucky number," you may tell someone. "In fact, every time I do a math problem, the answer comes up 7."

Before anyone has a chance to prove this is not so, begin this number trick.

"Choose a number," you tell your victim. "Any number. Just don't tell me what it is."

When this is done, you say, "Add 9 to the number you just chose."

"Now multiply that total by 2," you continue, when the addition is completed.

"Subtract 4 from the number you got when you multiplied," you say for the next step.

"Divide that answer by 2," you suggest next.

The trick is nearly finished now. For the last step you direct, "Subtract the number you started with."

Watch as the truth dawns on your victim. "See?" you will probably say. "What did I tell you? The answer is 7, isn't it?"

Let's practise this trick, just to make sure it works. Begin with number 20.

$$\begin{array}{r} ① \quad 20 \\ \text{add 9} \quad +\ 9 \\ \hline ② \quad 29 \times 2 = 58 \\ -\ 4 \\ \hline 2\ )\ \overline{54} \\ \hline 27 \\ -20 \\ \hline 7 \end{array}$$

How about that?

Five Is a Tricky Number

This quick mental math trick works every time.

Have your victim write a number on a piece of paper.

"Now add 7 to that number," you say.

"Take the total you just got and multiply that by 2," you command for the next step.

"Now subtract 4 from the product when you multiplied."

When this is done, you tell your victim, "Divide the subtraction answer by 2."

"Subtract the number you started with," you continue.

When the math work is all finished, pretend to think for a few seconds. Then grin and announce, "Your final answer is 5."

This is always true with this tricky number problem when the math is done correctly. Let's zip through it just to see that it works.

Starting with:

$$
\begin{array}{r}
12 \\
+\ 7 \\
\hline
19 \times 2 = \ 38 \\
-\ 4 \\
\hline
2\ )\ \overline{34} \\
\hline
17 \\
-12 \\
\hline
5
\end{array}
$$

Memorize the commands. Then try this one on your math teacher!

TRICKS THAT SEEM IMPOSSIBLE

Changing Places

Set up 2 quarters and a nickel on a table top or desk as shown here.

25¢   5¢   25¢

Tell your victim, "I am going to move the right-hand quarter so that it is between the nickel and the quarter on the left."

"What's so difficult about that?" your victim will ask.

"I am not going to move the nickel. What's more I won't touch the left-hand quarter."

By now, you have everyone watching you keenly.

"Can you move the right-hand quarter?"

"Yes."

"Can you tip the table?"

"No. And I won't shake the table either or hit it."

"Can you touch the nickel?"

"Yes, but I won't move it."

"You can't move the nickel and can't touch the left-hand quarter?"

"That's right."

"There has to be a trick to it!"

A clever victim may suggest moving the quarter with a pencil or putting a piece of paper over it.

"That's touching it," you can tell the victim. "That quarter is only touched by the nickel and the tabletop."

You will soon be asked to perform the trick. Here it is: Put a finger down firmly on top of the nickel. Move the right-hand quarter an inch or so to the right with your free hand.

Then quickly slide that quarter to hit it hard against the side of the nickel. The nickel won't move but the quarter on the left will bounce an inch or so away from the nickel. That leaves plenty of room for you to put the right-hand quarter between the other 2 coins.

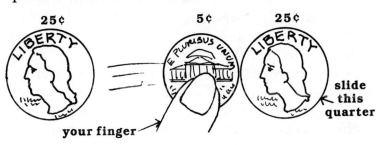

25¢   5¢   25¢

your finger →

slide this quarter

Without Lifting Your Pencil

Draw the square and circle shown below on a piece of paper. (Don't worry about making the square exactly square or the circle perfectly round.)

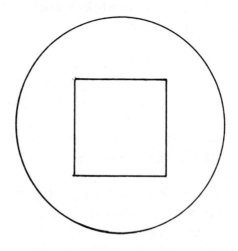

Show this drawing to your victim.

"I can draw this figure without lifting my pencil from the paper. Can you?"

Unless your friend knows the trick, there's no way to make such a drawing without lifting the pencil from the paper.

When you're asked to show the trick, it's really quite simple.

Draw the square without lifting your pencil. When you finish, keep the point of the pencil on the paper.

Now, fold a corner of the paper over until it

touches the edge of the pencil point. Slide the pencil point onto this folded paper. Continue drawing for about an inch along the folded paper. Let the pencil point slide off the folded part.

The pencil point is now on the original drawing about an inch from the square you drew first. Draw the circle now.

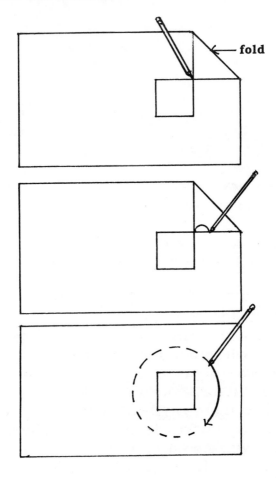

That's all there is to making the impossible easy.

The Reversing Arrow

Draw an arrow like the one shown below on a piece of paper or a file card. Make it good and dark and about an inch long.

Lean the paper or card against something so that it stands up with the arrow pointing to your right. Now you can set up your victim as you say:

"See how that arrow points to my right? I can make it look like it's pointing to my left!"

Here is an important part of this trick. You said you can make it "look" like the arrow points left. You did not say you would make it point left.

"I can do this without touching the paper or moving it in any way," you say.

Obviously, this sounds impossible. So your victim will probably ask a bunch of questions to pin you down.

You will not touch the paper?

You won't move the table?

You don't have to move the paper?

You won't go around and look through the paper from the other side?

When you are ready to spring the trap all you need to do is fill a glass with water. Place the glass in front of the arrow. Move the glass forward or backward until the arrow points left when you look at it through the water in the glass.

It's as simple as that. The glass full of water becomes a lens, which reverses the arrow when it's the proper distance from the paper or card. It also makes the arrow appear longer than it really is, by the way.

Stronger than It Looks

For this trick, you need a sheet of paper about 6 inches wide and eight inches long. Notebook paper will work just fine.

Place 2 glasses on a tabletop or desk so that they are 4 or 5 inches apart.

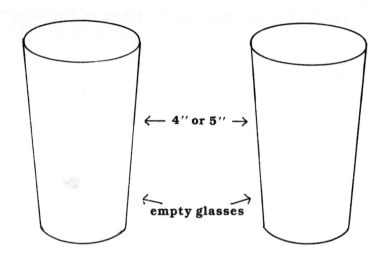

← 4" or 5" →

empty glasses

Partially fill a third glass with water and set it near the 2 empty glasses. Pretend to look carefully at the sheet of paper.

"You know, paper is a lot stronger than it looks."

Place the paper on top of the two glasses so that it reaches from one glass top to the other. By now you should have the attention of your victim or victims.

"In fact," (here you may hesitate a bit), "I think this paper is strong enough to hold up the glass with the water in it." You may want to point to the glass which is partially full of water so that there is no misunderstanding.

"Yes, I'm sure of it. This piece of paper is so strong, I know it will hold the third glass between the other 2."

Then the questions will begin. Stay cool and calm as you tell the rules.

"The glass of water will touch only the paper.

It won't rest on the rim of either of the other glasses. I won't move the other glasses. They will stay where they are. Even so, this piece of paper will hold the other glass up. The ends of the paper will touch the 2 glasses and there will not be any other supports.''

Unless someone in the group is really very clever, no one will guess how you can do this. When you have built up the trick enough, it's time to take the spotlight and start your act.

Begin by folding the paper in an accordion fold along the long side. It looks like this from either end:

Now, put the folded paper between the tops of the 2 glasses to make a "bridge." Very carefully, put the glass (with the water in it) on the folded paper. Be sure it is correctly balanced; then let go. The paper will support it.

Practise this trick to be sure you're doing it correctly. It isn't a bad idea to use a plastic glass to hold the water the first few times.

The Balancing Match

Stand a nickel on its side on top of a desk or tabletop. Then carefully balance a wooden kitchen match on the top edge of the nickel. It doesn't matter whether the match is new or used.

Since this balancing act is a trick all its own,

you may want to practise it a few times before performing the trick.

Now, place an empty glass upside down, over the coin and balanced match. Be careful not to hit the end of the match or your trick is over before you start. Make sure the glass is large enough so that the ends of the match don't touch the sides of the glass.

"Now," you say, "here is what I dare you to do. I challenge you to make the match fall off the top of the nickel. But the nickel must not fall over.

"You may not hit the table. You may not move the glass or hit it. It is not necessary to touch the table at all."

It won't take long before everyone decides this is impossible. (Everyone, that is, except you.) Let your victims puzzle over this one before showing them the trick.

All it takes is a comb made of hard rubber or some kind of plastic.

Run the comb through your hair a few times. This builds up a charge of static electricity on the comb's surface. Place one end of the comb near the end of the match and slowly move it. If you have enough static electricity built up, the match will begin to turn. As it turns, it will fall off the edge of the nickel. That's all there is to it.

Before performing this trick, practise it a few times. Unfortunately, some combs won't work. Try a few to find one that does. And if your hair is very short, you may have people volunteer their hair for combing!

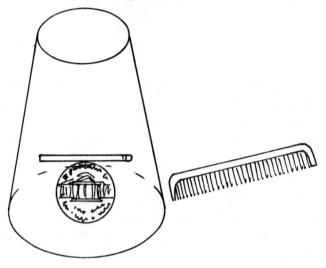

Surprising Balancing Act

Cut a circle about 3 inches in diameter out of a piece of cardboard. Don't worry if it isn't a perfect circle.

Poke a hole in the middle of the circle and push a wooden pencil about halfway through. Don't worry if the hole isn't exactly at the mid-point of the circle.

Now, pretend you're trying to balance the pencil and cardboard circle on the end of your finger. When it keeps falling off, try the side of your finger. Naturally, the pencil won't balance.

Move the cardboard closer to the pencil's point. Try again. It still won't balance.

Insist you can make it balance. Offer to let others try. They will fail.

Now is the time to show your brilliant skill.

"I'll just add weight. Heavier things are easier to balance," you say.

Carefully stick the tines of a dinner fork through the cardboard near one edge. Careful is the keynote here. First, you don't want to ruin the cardboard. Second, you don't want to cut your finger!

With the fork extending or hanging from the lower edge of the cardboard, you are now ready for a surprising balancing act.

Rest the pencil near the point on the side of your finger. Move it forward or backward until you can feel it balance. Let go and the whole thing will seem to hang in space.

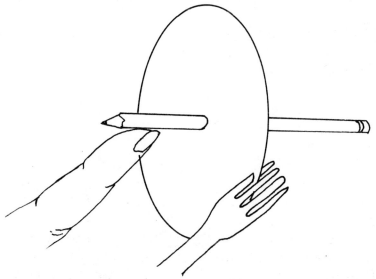

You can change the way this device balances by slipping the cardboard nearer or farther from the pencil's point.

If you want to improve this trick you may want to experiment with larger or smaller cardboard circles and longer or shorter pencils.

Showmanship—plus Balance

Many tricks take a little showmanship to make them successful. In this one, most of the showmanship comes at the end of the performance. Not only does this trick *sound* impossible, it *looks* impossible when you've done it!

You need 2 dinner forks, an empty drinking glass, and a half-dollar (fifty-cent piece). Oh, yes, don't forget the steady hands! If a half-dollar isn't handy, a quarter will work just as well. For that matter, you can use a cup or a mug, if you want, instead of a glass.

Begin by balancing the coin on the edge of the cup or glass—just to attract the attention of the onlookers. Then hold up the 2 forks, study the coin and glass, and begin your trickery with a talk:

"Someone told me it is possible to balance these 2 forks on that coin."

"Big deal," someone will probably reply.

"Yes, but I am supposed to do it so that only the coin touches the glass. The 2 forks may touch each other and they must touch the coin. But only the coin is allowed to touch the rim of the glass."

"That isn't so hard," your victim may reply.

"But only one edge of the coin is allowed to touch the rim of the glass. And the forks may not touch that edge of the coin."

At this point, you have your victims hooked. It is time to allow them to try this impossible balancing act.

After everyone else gives up, show your stuff. Slip the coin between the first and second tines of the 2 forks. This leaves the handles of the forks pointing away from each other. This leaves the handles of the forks pointing away from each other.

Here comes the tricky part—both for your audience and for you! Rest the edge of the coin on the rim of the glass so that the forks do not touch the glass. Carefully move the handles of the forks back and forth until the entire thing balances on the rim of the glass.

The coin will stick out from the glass and the forks will appear to hang out in space. As you work to achieve a balance, you'll feel the proper place to hold the forks. This feeling will be in your fingers when you realize you no longer have to support the coin and forks.

Practise this trick before you show it. It takes steady hands and a little work, but it's worth it. Even when people see this balancing act, it's hard for them to believe their eyes.

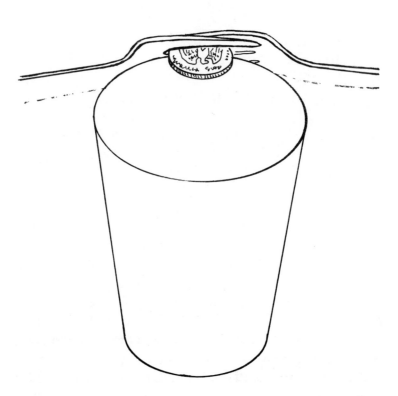

The Pickup Stunt

For this trick you need a table-tennis ball and a glass. The glass must have a bulge in the middle (see the sketch) or at the bottom. Place the ball under the glass on top of a table. Then stand back to admire your work, setting the stage for the stunt.

"Can you lift that ball off the table without touching anything besides the glass?" you ask. Go on to set a few rules. "But you can't slide the glass off the table so the ball falls to the floor. You must lift the ball, not drop it."

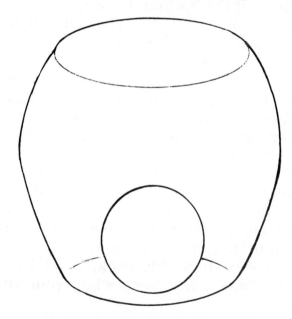

Like many good tricks, at first glance this one seems impossible, too. (Actually, it continues to look impossible at second or even third glance!)

Someone may try to lift the ball using static electricity from a comb, but this probably won't work. The ball is too heavy for that.

When showdown time arrives and your reputation is on the line, get a firm hold on the glass. Begin to rotate it on the top of the table. This will cause the ball to begin to circle the rim of the glass. Move the glass more quickly and the ball will pick up speed.

As the ball speeds up, it will start to climb the side of the glass. Since the glass bulges out wider in the middle than at the opening, the ball will begin to spin around the bulge.

By the way, don't even bother trying this trick with a glass which does not bulge in the middle or at the bottom. It won't work.

By now you will find you can move the glass back and forth in rapid little shakes of your hand and the ball will spin inside.

Gently lift the glass while you keep shaking it. The spinning ball comes off the table with the glass. You can continue shaking the glass and the ball will continue spinning until your hand gets tired.

A marble will also work in this trick. So will a small rubber, plastic or wooden ball. Just be sure to practise this trick in private until you know exactly how to get the ball spinning fast enough to lift it from the table.

When you show this trick, don't be overly modest. Take a few bows when your show is over.

Coin Push

If you don't mind getting downright sneaky, this quick trick is sure to catch someone. Like so many nasty little stunts, this one depends upon the use of words. People hearing it think one thing, while you have something else in mind.

You need an object, such as a quarter or a spoon, and a ring. Hold up the ring and then place it next to the coin or spoon. Then say:

"I can push that coin through this ring" or, "I am sure I can push the spoon through the ring."

Let your victim examine both objects. Obviously, you have lost what little mind you once had, he or she may be thinking.

"I can do it," you insist.

When your friend insists you can't, it is time to get the show on the road.

Hold the ring in one hand next to the coin or spoon you are going to push. Stick one of the fingers of your other hand through the ring. Give the coin or spoon a push. That's all that is necessary.

You may wish to add, "I just pushed the coin through the ring," but you probably won't have to explain yourself. The look on your victim's face usually lets you know you have scored again.

QUICK TRICKS

Never Seen Before and Never Seen Again

This trick has been around for hundreds of years. It probably first began as a riddle. Then someone turned the riddle into a trick.

Tell someone, "In just a minute I'll show you something no one living has ever seen before. After I have shown it to you no one will ever see it again."

This sounds pretty spooky. Naturally, your victim has to be interested.

Crack the shell of a nut of any kind. A peanut is great since you can crack its thin shell in your fingers.

Hold up the nut inside. "See this. No one has ever seen it before."

Then quickly eat the nut. Once you have swallowed it, you can finish the trick.

"And now, no one will ever see it again."

Never mind the groans. You told the truth!

Easy
Under

Place one coin on top of a desk or table. Hand a second coin to the person you've chosen to be your victim.

"It's easy to place this coin under the one on the table," you tell your victim. "I can do it without moving the coin on the table or even touching it."

It won't take most victims long before they are willing to admit defeat.

Take the coin in one hand and hold it under the table or desk.

"Now it is under the coin on the table," you can tell them. Of course, the victim already sees that he or she has been duped. Explaining your success may not be necessary.

There is an even sneakier variation of this stunt. After putting one coin on top of the table, you say, "It's easy to place this second coin under the one on the table. You may not touch the coin on the table. *But* you may hit the table on its top or its side, if you want."

Just be sure you're using a strong, heavy table. It's fun to watch your victims try to get the coin to bounce high enough for them to slide the other coin under it. Of course, it won't work!

When in Rome . . .

One of the best things the Romans did for us was to give us Roman numerals. This system of writing numbers helps you invent some great tricks!

Here's an example: Write this equation on a piece of paper. Write it really large—even though it's wrong. It should be easy to see.

$$XI + I = X$$

Be sure your victim knows the equation is *wrong*. You may even want to mutter, "Eleven plus one does not equal 10. But I know this equation is correct."

If your friend happens to spot the error before you make that comment, you may say, "It just looks wrong. I know it's right. I just wrote it."

As soon as your friendly opponent insists the equation is wrong, it's time to make your pitch:

"I can correct it. I won't touch the paper. I won't erase anything on the paper. No one will have to change the paper in any way. Yet the equation will be correct."

This seems impossible. Most people will suggest you have just misplaced your mind.

When you are ready to show your stuff, casually walk to the other side of the table. Look! You now see the original equation upside down. It looks like this: X = I + IX (10 = 1 + 9)

It *is* correct. How about that?

Three into Four

This quick brain buster is a good trick. You can do it without any preparation. If your victims catch on, congratulate them. If no one sees through the trick, your reputation as a tricky person blossoms.

Place 3 matches or toothpicks or even drinking straws on a tabletop.

"Can you make these 3 things into 4?" you ask. "You may not bend or break or cut or damage any of the 3." (You can substitute the name of your chosen object for things.)

If you're really sure of yourself and want to get someone's goat you might add, "The average second-grader does this in 32 seconds." Then start counting seconds.

If your victim fails, everyone laughs at a person who could not beat a second-grader. If he or she is successful, so what? Anybody should be able to do better than a second-grader.

Here's the simple solution. Making 3 objects into 4 is a snap—either way.

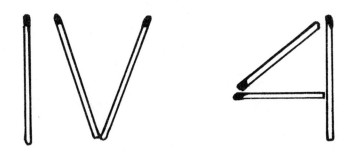

Paper Puff

Tear 3 or 4 pieces of paper so that they're about the size of postage stamps. Place them on the back of your hand.

Tell your victims, "I'm going to blow all but one of these papers off my hand in one big puff. Just to make it harder, I want you to choose the piece of paper that I won't blow off."

Encourage them to pick the papers up and look at them carefully. Let them rearrange the papers on your hand. The one rule is that the papers may not touch each other. (This means, certainly, that they may not be stacked on top of each other.)

When the one paper is selected, it's time for you to prove you can do what you claim—and you can!

Here's the trick. Put the index finger of your free hand down firmly on the paper that is to remain in place. Then blow.

The other pieces of paper flutter away and the chosen one remains.

Remember to pick up the fallen paper. People may forgive you for tricking them, but nobody likes a litterbug.

Carrying Water in a Tissue

Set up this trick by pulling a facial tissue out of its box. Pretend to examine it very carefully.

"These tissues are really strong," you can say to begin. "I think this tissue is much stronger than it looks."

Show the tissue to your intended victim. "Can you see how close together those fibres are."

Then, as though the thought just struck, you add, "I think I can carry water in this tissue. Don't you think so?"

Of course, your victim doesn't think so. How ridiculous even to consider carrying water in a facial tissue!

If your victim says it's impossible, offer to prove

111

that it can be done. Should your victim think it is possible, ask him or her to show you how. Either way, you've got your trick going.

Since water is usually found in the kitchen—that's the place to go. When a person pours or runs water into a facial tissue the result is a soggy mess. So what else is new?

To prove your point, take the tissue in one hand. Open the refrigerator's freezer door and take out an ice cube. Wrap the cube in the tissue and carry it across the room. It's as simple as that.

If your victim protests, ask, "What is ice?"

The only possible answer is, "Frozen water."

If that's not good enough, hand the ice cube to your friend.

"Hold onto this for a few minutes. When it starts to melt you'll have all the water you want."

That should be all it takes. You've won again.

Now You See It— Now You Don't

Even when they know they are being set up for a trick, most people can't resist joining in.

When you hold up a card or a bracelet or any small object and pretend to study it, people wonder what you are up to.

"You know, I can make this become invisible," you say. Turn the object and look at it from another angle. "Actually, I can make this item invisible to you but not to the others in the room." You look directly at your newest victim when you speak.

This can't be so. "No way," your victim will say to you. Then he or she will probably add, "You're trying to trick me, aren't you?"

Just smile and shrug. "There's only one way to find out."

Someone will ask that you demonstrate.

"Here is how it works," you can tell them. "I will make this object invisible to one person but not to the rest of us. It will be invisible as long as that person stays here in this room."

The catch is disgustingly simple. Put the card or whatever on top of the victim's head. Expect others to moan and groan. It does not matter. You've done what you said you'd do.

Just don't play this trick in a room where the victim can look into a mirror.

Two Cookies, Two Caps, One Trick

"I have magic powers," is one way to introduce this stunt. "I can put 2 things under 2 baseball caps. Then I can eat the 2 things. Afterwards, I can put them back under one of the 2 caps."

Expect some rude remarks when you make this claim. You may pretend to be offended and make some great statement, such as, "That's gross! Ugh."

When you're told to put up or shut up, the trick is easy. Place one cookie or one cracker under each of 2 caps.

"I have now put 2 things under 2 caps," you may explain. (This way, even the slowest member of the group stays with the stunt.)

Remove the caps and eat the cookies. You may even say something such as, "Um. Good."

It is not necessary, but you can now explain, "See, I have eaten the two things."

Finally, put on one of the caps. Smile—and wait for applause.

Do you have to tell your victims you have now put the 2 things under one of the caps? Surely, they aren't that slow, or are they?

REALLY NASTY TRICKS

Underwater Challenge

A good way to start this trick is to fill a tall glass with water. Then, when everyone is watching, drop a coin into the water.

After the coin has settled to the bottom of the glass, you state your challenge:

"I am going to set this glass on the table. If you can get the coin out without spilling any of the water in the glass, the coin is yours."

There has to be a way to do this. You can expect a victim to volunteer.

"There is just one catch," you continue. "I want your word that once you begin you won't quit. No one likes a quitter!"

So who is going to quit without getting that coin? By now your victim is all but diving into the glass for the coin.

"One last warning. I am going to set the glass on the table in a special way. Are you still sure you want to do this? I would hate to be responsible for turning you into a quitter."

By now, you have made such a thing about of being a quitter there is not a way in the world your victim will back down. Therefore, it is once again sly time.

You need a piece of fairly stiff paper. Notebook paper works just fine. A piece about 4 by 5 inches or so is great.

Cover the open mouth of the glass with the paper. Hold the paper firmly in place. Invert the glass so that the paper and open end of the glass are down.

Give the water just a second or 2 to wet the paper. Now, being as careful as you have ever been in your life, it is time to remove your hand.

Without moving the paper even a fraction of an inch, hold the glass just above the tabletop. As you slip your fingers away from the paper, ease the glass onto the table. Not one drop of water will leak out, if you do this carefully.

What you now have looks like this.

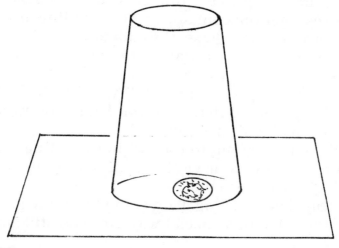

By the way, don't set this up on top of a table-cloth or place mat. If you do, the cloth will become a wet sponge and your victim will die laughing as you clean up the mess.

Now comes the tricky part. Slowly, and with care, you must slip the paper out from under the glass of water. Hold the glass with one hand and remove the paper with the other. If you lose a few drops of water just clean them up with a cloth.

Then, with a wave of your hand, present the glass and coin to your victim.

"Give it your best shot," you may wish to say. "Just remember the rules. Don't spill any water. And don't give up."

Which Coin Did You Give Me?

This stunt has been frustrating victims for years. It is a play on words that begins with the victim expecting some sort of magic trick. It ends with the victim more than just a little bit upset.

Tell someone you have a very special coin trick. To demonstrate this trick you need 2 coins of the same denomination: 2 dimes or 2 quarters or 2 whatever. Once the victim hands you the 2 coins you are ready to begin.

"Look closely at these 2 coins," you command.

The victim does so, naturally.

"You are going to have to identify these coins again in just a second or 2. You may even want to check the dates and mint marks," you say.

After your victim is positive he or she can identify the coins, you place them in one of your hands. Put that hand behind your back along with your other hand. Pass the coins back and forth once or twice. If you want to create suspense you can do this for quite some time. You may even wish to mumble some magic words.

Eventually, hold one coin in each hand. Bring both hands out in front of you. Hold them, palms up, and open them.

"Now," you tell your victim, "tell me which of these 2 coins you just gave me."

Certainly, you were given both the coins. Your victim knows this and so do you.

"I gave you both of them!" is the natural reaction.

It is your turn to look puzzled. "Are you certain? Look carefully at them. Are you positive you gave me both of these coins?"

"Yes. Of course I am certain." This or something close to this is what you can expect as an answer.

"If you are sure you gave me both of these coins, why thanks. I appreciate the gift!" Smile—and put the coins in your pocket. Watch your victim's face as he or she realizes your play on words is the only trick involved.

Whether you actually keep the coins your victim "gave" to you is up to you. You may lose a friend. You may get punched in the nose. Or your victim may have a good laugh and go looking for victims to play the trick on.

Tricky Trap

Some people just seem to beg to be put down. You know the ones. They boast and brag and act as if they know more than anyone else.

Tricky Trap is designed for just this sort of character. It works best when a few other people are around to see you put one over on the loudmouth.

Fill 2 glasses a little more than half full of water. (If you want to be on the safe side, use unbreakable glasses.) Make a real drama out of filling and checking the water level in the glasses. The amount of water really doesn't matter, but when you pretend it does, you build the interest of your audience.

Once you're satisfied with the amount of water in the glasses, it's time to set up your victim.

"This trick needs steady hands and real concentration," you may begin. "Not everyone is up to it. In fact, I don't want any people to volunteer to try it unless they're absolutely sure they're going to be able to hold these glasses without spilling the water in them."

What big shot can turn down a challenge like that? When your victim assures you he or she is the one for the job, you're on the way.

"Hold out both hands, palms down," you command.

Carefully, place one glass on the back of each hand.

"Can you hold these?" Act as if you're afraid your victim lacks the strength to hold the glasses.

"Are you positive you can hold them without spilling even a drop?"

Your victim is certain, naturally. This is a snap.

"Great!" Smile at your victim and walk away.

It may take a minute or so for the realization to sink in, but your victim is in the Tricky Trap. How do you go about getting 2 glasses of water off the backs of your hands without spilling a drop? It doesn't help when everyone in the room is laughing at you.

What happens is pretty much up to you. You may want to take this poor loudmouth off the hook and remove the glasses yourself. Or you may decide to let him or her work it out alone.

Is That Worth a Quarter?

This nasty little trick is really a play on words. It's a great put-down for people who deserve to be put in their place.

Pretend you're trying to tear a sheet of notebook paper into 4 equal pieces. (You can turn this into a real production, if you want.) Fold the paper into fourths. Then crease each fold. Work at making the paper tear along each crease. Yet no matter how hard you try, one of the tears always leaves the crease.

Fooling around with the paper, you may make this a quick stunt or drag it out for several minutes. At any rate, your victim will eventually get into the act, and then it's easy for you to set it up.

Pretend to be indignant and upset. "So you think it is easy to tear a paper into fourths. Well, it isn't."

Your victim will probably insist there's nothing to it.

"I'll tell you what," you can exclaim. "If you can tear a sheet of paper into 4 pieces the same size, I'll give you a quarter. But I don't think you can do it."

Now there's a challenge no one can turn down. When your victim hands you the required pieces of paper, be sure to say what a fine job of tearing it was.

"You tore the paper into exact quarters," you can say. Hand one of the pieces to your victim. "Here is the quarter I promised you ."

Of course, a quarter of the paper was not what was expected. It is also true that you have kept your tricky word.

Three Can't Be Four

Are you the sort of trick-player who won't stop at anything? Are you the type of person who never gets bothered by how sneaky a trick may be? Do you enjoy really irritating your friends? If so, this trick is for you!

Hold 3 quarters in one hand. Look at them and remark, "These 4 quarters are all just a little different, aren't they?" Hold the 3 quarters towards your victim.

Naturally, your victim will say something, such as, "There are only 3 quarters in your hand."

Pretend to be surprised. Hold up the quarters

and study them with care. "Are you sure? Did you say 3? I see 4."

Since you have a reputation as a trickster, your victim knows something is coming. Even so, he or she will insist there are only 3 quarters in your hand.

Rattle the quarters around in your closed fist and check again. "I see 4."

By now, it has become something of a crusade for your victim. There are only 3 quarters in your hand. Your friend is absolutely certain about that.

How long you wish to continue the debate is up to you. It also depends on how long your victim will put up with such nonsense.

You can decide when the time has come to spring the trap.

"I still see 4 quarters in my hand. You think there are only 3. Look, if you're so positive, will you give me another quarter if I'm wrong?"

By now, your victim is ready to do battle. If you have set the stage properly, and if your victim reacts as most people do, the answer will come quickly.
"Yes—sure."

At this point most people don't really listen to what you say to them. They are intent on the quarters in your hand.

"Well, I am wrong. You are right. There are only 3 quarters in my hand. Since I am wrong, you owe me the quarter you just promised."

You may need to review what you said about getting another quarter if you are wrong. Even then you probably won't collect the quarter. But no matter whether you get the quarter or not, you have added one more success to your score.

The Severed Finger

This trick is what people sometimes call a "heart stopper." This is because victims are so surprised they may think their hearts have either stopped or have leaped right up into their throats.

To make The Severed Finger work, you have to do some careful preparation. The first step is to find a small cardboard box that's about 4 inches wide, 6 inches long and an inch or so deep. don't worry about finding one exactly that size—just come close.

Cut a hole in the bottom of the box as shown in the drawing. This hole should be just big enough so that your index or middle finger will fit through it.

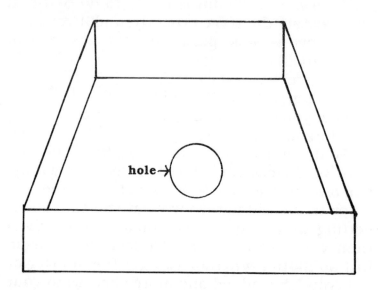

Use clean white cloth to make a nest in the bottom of the box. Poke your finger through the hole and arrange the cloth around it so that it looks as if your finger is lying in the box. Cover the entire bottom of the box carefully, so there's no sign of the hole.

Now that most of your finger seems to be lying in the box on white cloth, you can add some makeup to give it a really repulsive look. A little bit of rouge will make the finger look as though traces of blood are sticking to it. Some face powder or blusher rubbed into the finger gives it a dead look.

Put the lid back on the box and hold it with your other hand under it. This keeps your victims from realizing your finger is poked through the bottom.

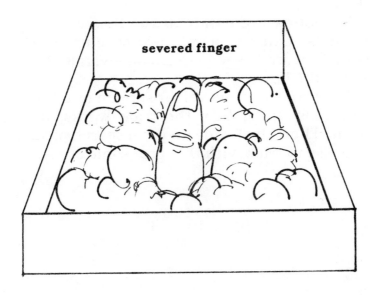
severed finger

To make this trick work, you have to give it a good buildup. Be sure to look solemn and serious. You can begin like this.

"There was a terrible car accident in front of our house last night. Three people had to be taken to the hospital."

Now that you have the victim's attention you can really develop your story.

"One of the children got her finger cut off. There was a lot of blood and she cried and cried."

Pause just a second or two to let your words sink in.

"After everyone was gone I found her finger. It was lying in the grass. Since I didn't know what to do with it I put it in the freezer last night. I have it here in this box. What do you think I should do with it?"

Pull the top off the box. There is a human finger lying all bloody and pale in the bottom of the box.

Let your victim stare at the finger for a few seconds. Usually people are so curious they bend forward to see better. Then wiggle the finger in the box.

After your victims yell or scream or faint you can show them how the trick works, if you want. Then all of you can go in search of someone else to trick with this gruesome stunt.

Index